[The Way a Line Hallucinates Its Own Linearity]

[[The Way a Line Hallucinates Its Own Linearity]]

————

POEMS

Danielle Vogel

Red Hen Press | *Pasadena, CA*

Book design by Mark E. Cull

Library of Congress Cataloging-in-Publication Data

Names: Vogel, Danielle, author.
Title: The way a line hallucinates its own linearity / Danielle Vogel.
Description: First edition. | Pasadena, CA : Red Hen Press, [2020]
Identifiers: LCCN 2019043376 (print) | LCCN 2019043377 (ebook) | ISBN
    9781597098212 (trade paperback) | ISBN 9781597098229 (ebook)
Subjects: LCGFT: Poetry.
Classification: LCC PS3622.O345 W39 2020 (print) | LCC PS3622.O345
    (ebook) | DDC 811/.6—dc23
LC record available at https://lccn.loc.gov/2019043376
LC ebook record available at https://lccn.loc.gov/2019043377

The National Endowment for the Arts, the Los Angeles County Arts Commission, the Ahmanson
Foundation, the Dwight Stuart Youth Fund, the Max Factor Family Foundation, the Pasadena
Tournament of Roses Foundation, the Pasadena Arts & Culture Commission and the City of Pasadena
Cultural Affairs Division, the City of Los Angeles Department of Cultural Affairs, the Audrey &
Sydney Irmas Charitable Foundation, the Kinder Morgan Foundation, the Meta & George Rosenberg
Foundation, the Allergan Foundation, the Riordan Foundation, Amazon Literary Partnership, and
the Mara W. Breech Foundation partially support Red Hen Press.

First Edition
Published by Red Hen Press
www.redhen.org

Thank you,

to the editors of *Caketrain*, the *Denver Quarterly*, *Puerto del Sol*, *Sidebrow*, *Small Po[r]tions*, and *Tarpaulin Sky* where earlier versions of these poems first appeared.

to all at Red Hen Press.

to Akilah Oliver, my mentor and friend, for asking, "What are the limits of the body?" during a class at Naropa University in the summer of 2007.

to Anne Waldman, Elizabeth Robinson, and Selah Saterstrom for their close mentorship.

to HR Hegnauer, Yanara Friedland, Richard Froude, Sara Renee Marshall, and Jessica Schnabel for helping me hold the many transformations of this book over the years.

to my family, chosen and given.

to Renee Gladman, for every second.

and, to you, Dear Reader, this book is the second in a triptych of poetic texts: *Between Grammars* (Noemi, 2015), *The Way a Line Hallucinates Its Own Linearity* and, the eventual *A Library of Light*. While each overflows into the next, they can be read alone or in any order. Thank you for being here with me.

[CONTENTS]

What is the primary duty of repair?

—Akilah Oliver

[Displacements]

Dear Reader,

even in the most lightless of places, we are able to dig up sensation through sound.

Here, a clutch of syllables tied with blue string—red clover, lavender, damiana, juniper berries, and deer's tongue. A black candle. A copper ring of hair. Ink. Let it warp.

Into this. A humming. Pulled. And then. Away. Say, *spark*. Say, *flare*. Your hands, a looping. Lip skin. Eyelash. Elbow. Stitch me into place.

Come here with a register of questions. Bolts of color. A serrated knife. A willingness to fillet. To realign. Un-hem and then seam again.

Hum for me. One key.

To gather these tiny omissions. All things that belong to me. A door in the stars. A door in the tongue. To have slipped—

Dear Reader, this book is a séance. Here, we are all talking. The *I*. The *she*. Oscillating within. What we carry conjoins.

Between us we'll create another sustainable self. A communal body existing in the wake of an absent one.

My hands. Up to your mouth. And all of this happens. Take the word. Hold it until it pieces. I feel the sentence you are moving.

Dear Reader, all pages architecture intimacy. The symbiotic bonds between this space and ourselves. What happened. What wasn't remembered.

A self that was once uninhabitable. A childhood coiled up like some shame shed. Until this body arrived in the present as if for the first time. Through its being read, it was written. I wanted it.

The contortions that language allows. To bring us here, netted. To slow the space and compose a body between us. How these words appear sanitary and contained but how, just like us, they are multiplying subdermally.

Dear Reader, this small sentence is the hallucinatory sill. I once turned out the lights and invited you to make love to me. *Please*, I said. And turned over onto my belly and waited. I moved slowly, undoing my legs. I imagined the springs and foam would sort themselves into shape, that you would feel the weight of me and appear. I let you hear me breathing.

Dear Reader, these are porous sheets.

Here, within the communal lung of the word. We pulp language through its syntax. An irregular net, a nervous system, levitating, linking us through the book. Lead with your own breath pawing.

The body rises synesthetically. Saturated and liquidic. The emergence of sound through a lid of skin.

A willingness to hold and be held. This narrative: language looking while I transfuse.

Negotiate the body through noise. What these collated spaces suggest. As we re-imagine the place of the page so that it may exist.

Dear Reader, I write the gauziness of that grainy opened
envelope upon unopened envelope of recollecting—

The way the body halos. A voice attached by some
accident. All these gestures. An inscriptive surface. The
skin. Graphed. The inner duration.

Look hard. The trajectory of a horizontal line—seemingly
contained. Its solitary linearity. A second line crosses the
first. A third and fourth. A latticework. Correspondents
in their adjacency, a tension develops between strands.
Somehow still maintaining their separate linearites, they
converse, bisect, and fragment one another, creating a new,
interrupted unity.

In our crossing, there is a difference between a knot and
a clasp. Our natures dovetail in the catching. A knot,
the thickened tissue of a thing, unconcerned with what
extends from its knobby enclosure.

A clasp, contingent. Imaging a line, disrupted, restored
again. Hoop of a memory, spliced and re-cinched.

We breach the noun of a thing to verb it. It still needs our
body.

There is a slowness. Gathering bolts of wet color. What asks to be rises in light. The translation of a color as it becomes another. As its pigment leans and weakens, making way.

I used to think I was interested in dislocation only, but it may be that I am writing toward a buoyancy I have not yet learned to create.

A hatched grid. Amniotic sound and light. The gift of a tongue reshaping language. So that the form appears in the wake of its vocabulary.

However transitory our materials. To find her. The flexed linear network of the alphabet. A grid into which we've fitted the swings.

Dear Reader, the body knows what the voice cannot. The remnants, residual, deep in the tissue. The pleasure of inversions. Let's let her through the fissures.

Sentences can do that. They can take a girl. The vertigo of the sentence of the girl.

Dear Reader, I imagine you arriving.

When you are here, everything happens in small spaces.
Your eye is a mirror. We flicker in. Our hands land again.

To hear them talk. The hands. Where they've been. The
unbuckled palm. The cockling hull, shingled. A break in
the line.

Each hand is a book. Handle her. The series stored, unstored. Her casing to uncover. Her handles. Marked.

The hand holds things. In the muscle, is memory. Dredged, scaled, a little fish gill. Little lipless hand. Little widowed hand.

It sees in slippages. How to deal with the things that must be. We start at the spaces cleaved.

There is the hip. The blade. The wrist. The button. There is the knob of the joint. The brain. The tongue. The clavicle. The ribs. They are all handles, holds, keyholes, baskets.

Through the crisis of her having had a self that would not appear. She threads her thinking. The strands of her having seen, spoken, somewhere, at some time, accrues.

Dear Reader, we begin inside and outside of words.
Uncovered, the dark scribbles. It only takes one letter on
the page and we are already inside one another's lungs.
Time splayed through the sentence. A line contorted,
but linking nonetheless. Swatches of sound, overlaid.
You can't look without converging.

Dear Reader, this, a buckle cinching the gap between
what I can't say and what you can imagine.

We are raising place. *Where* is impossible to say. But if we
hold the word *arm* between us, a fifth arm appears.

If moving is defined by trajectory, if seeing by form,
then this line we both straddle materializes somewhere.
Without form and with it. We see from these inky
nodes. A toddler's body. A teenager's. A woman's. A man
stepping off a bus. Can appear here as if for the first time.
Over again, we fill their lungs.

Say *touch*, and we can't. But we can see from our oscillation between the two- and three-dimensional. We confront the invisible body. As one enters, burrowing from within toward an outside. And then in reverse. Through a vocabulary at once amorphous and continuous. We organize.

These lines pulling the cloth-wrapped curves of her. A rustling within the page milks her skin. A woman, an after-image.

Dear Reader, speech kicks. Webbing us. Across a tremorous light. Across a third skin worn about two bodies. Until the tongue becomes something. A lick for an unsealed envelope. The words, the bones, after. Sometimes you were so close, she would crumple and slur. A warming sap at the back of me.

Dear Reader, the book is a mammal the girl travels through. Pressing words. In contra. Hip-deep. In sound. In light. The organism of the page as it senses sound.

Dear Reader, language is a sensing organ. Treading sound through your throat, the body dilates. She's ashamed, but she wants a grammar. Let her unhook your mouth.

To meet you among its tow.

[Grieving Miniatures]

And the decay that has occurred below the body-ground—
this is what is carried

1.

[clasp of]   [tents]   [and]
[light   ]
[like a]   [fur]

At night, adjacent to the open window. Until the house quiets her twin bed and her mouth is against the thin metal grid of the window's screen. Space, embedded. Sight, a grating. She in every square and crossing. At every threshold of the pattern. Even after releasing, her face remembers the lattice. And it feels like someone is responding

2.

[whose responsibility]   [is]
[childhood]   [the project]
[of a]   [body]

Within a grid there are innumerable geometric possibilities.
To synchronize the volume of her. Line beside line. The
crossing begins. Between vision and an empirical body,
there is speech. Perceptions overlay. An interlocution of
lines that set her vibrating.

3.

[here]   [how it]   [this]
[holding]   [the lips]   [they]
[thought]   [i was]   [be-
cause i had]   [because]   [they
]   [had]   [hauled me   ]

Up close, the neurological field of the page, shot through, in its breathing. That synapse between there and here is diaphanous. The ink aggregates and gleams. As if its atomic makeup cannot settle, so instead makes room. She puts her left ear to the paper and watches her childhood hand write her name. An irregular net of sound—a nervous system—reorganizes.

4.

[until]   [all that is]
[is   involuntary   ]

This is an act for shelter. A series of entanglements to segment her into space. To hold her. The lines of her alphabet, appearing slowly. The clasps of her wait. Those places of intersection grieve and secrete.

5.

[he]   [was he]   [was a]
[but he]   [but he was not]

To fit inside a word's compartment. She leans into its
resonance. A body beside its design. Her voice strokes, a
series of machinations pawing the air around her.

6.

[i am]   [my own]   [an]
[of   ]

A shaping image, a receptacle of energy. Single continuous lines, dendritic, woven. The vocal noise that makes something human—its slick residuum. She is writing ropes. Catenary shapes, a suspension bridge, a transference of voices.

7.

[care take a poor]   [but]
[i've]   [never]   [been]
[able   ]

The spectra that lines overlaid allow. Between *form* and *from* are fine precise weavings. A mutation of threads. A stretched skin composed along the directional lines— nodal and major—of an alphabet.

8.

[neck to]   [navel a]   [

shrugging off]   [this]   [

wasn't]   [my]   [body]   [

to   heed   ]

These partial architectures of her. The writing accrues; it becomes easy to wonder *where* one is. Taut and doubled, this letter secured, invisibly, from the body's floor to the ceiling of its sound.

9.

[where they've]   [and how]
[i'll never]   [the]   [morning
so]   [sudden]   [the]   [
humming]   [has nowhere]

The loops of her script become places of congestion. These inverted, embedded things in the basket language creates. She runs her finger along the line. Everything is held as it passes.

10.

[hands]   [into]   [sound]
[sunk]   [my fingertips]   [to
the   tongue   ]

Even silence has its tonalities. That rift between thought and shape, between the idea of a thing and its enacted desire. Something to pass over one's skin: sounds when the object is indistinct.

11.

[against]   [a]   [bloating]
[sounds]   [the floor]   [a
slow]   [quaking]   [holds the
bones   ]   [in   ]

In the fluctuation between words and blankness is the
occasional drift of her hand.

12.

[as]   [thin as]   [a thread]
[of air]   [emptying]

The manifest and hidden are interlaced. Multidirectional planes, vanishing points at the periphery of a sentence. We are within an abstraction that yields.

13.

[the open rectangle]   [of a]
[door how]   [a]   [voice]
[opens]   [the dark]

All letters are occupied with touch. Their overall membranes faltering, activate the body. A dynamic field. A flat surface, given volume through geometry.

14.

[to]   [think]   [you are]   [

not]   [your other]   [self]

[but this]   [one]

To share the common wall of a book. A room floating in a
sentence.

15.

[to shelter up]   [its]   [

slats]   [to]   [organize]   [

my   ]   [fright   ]

Sight inscribes radiance. Particles sound, a pulsing space, a layering of each letter radiates. And here, what is. The kinetic transfer between verbs. Between humans. An always-present tense of encounter, unsheltering, all in transit toward the holding space.

16.

[throat my hips]   [your]   [
hook]   [your legs]   [
milky]   [my spine]   [can not
]   [exist]   [when the light
goes   ]

I am assembling the prospect of this page: the impossible tense of this relation is the present one. A page holds space for something begun. In the past, continued. To vigil: the present perfect progressive. The present continuous.

17.

[to account for]   [the turning]
[in]   [the]   [lungs]

The accumulation of lines vibrate in the eye. The tracing of letters holding space for movement. Physical mapping. Fields of energy, being seen, recognized. Transmitted and transformed.

18.

[and ambiguous]   [to lay my]
[sight or]   [sound]   [over a
]   [thing to keep]   [it]

But how to account for the moments between paragraphs?
All that remains in the lungs even after writing. Even after
the most forcible expiration possible.

19.

[syllable]   [taken up]   [into
]   [cords]

Even when the mouth wants to reject language as a replacement for what is lost. When experience no longer fits inside a sentence. To still believe in vocabulary's inflammatory response.

20.

[a low]   [circle]   [the

middle]   [a taper]   [into the

flickering   ]

Between language and the unutterable. A poetics of disorientation. She would like to make a mark that establishes the event of having lost, of having never been able, but there are no formal grieving ceremonies for a living body.

21.

[had]   [and]   [also]
[and   ]

The minute rifts between a voice and its body. The tentative lines, segmented. All the helixes of her thinking, bisected and divided into a spectrum. All the ways a line hallucinates its own linearity.

22.

[of]   [else]   [someplace

emptying   ]

This most insistent pressure. The body's refraction. The voice's. How they ridge, crosshatch, and section again. The disassociated self cannot be approached as an object. It cannot be laid out before us at the mouth of a room. The best we can do is trail its impressions.

23.

[where do you]   [your
alphabet i]   [could fold]   [
into   under   ]   [i]

A deferred center is a working of nets. This lattice distributes
the weight. The evanescence, shaped. Light emitted from
the weave. Threads of voice, and her body vibrates like a
curtain.

[A Residual Volume]

———

It has taken me twenty-three years. It has taken me thirty. Thirty-one years have taken me. To meet you. In the space of this page. In the place of this. It could be a room, as it has four walls, and there could be an island, as I am on one now. It is 4:35 a.m. It is 5:32, here, in the present, a waning gibbous hangs to the south of me, the robins have begun, and half a decade has receded.

To find a new throat from which to speak, the esophagus sheds its skin. I am writing you from three cities, from the north fork of an island, upon a winter's beach, upon a boat, at a sea-glass-colored table. I am writing you from the future. I am writing you from my childhood bedroom. I am climbing from its window down into your arms. And the screen catches my nightshirt. And the grass is wet, but I'll lie on it anyway. And the man steps off the bus again, at daybreak, during a snowstorm. This book in my mouth, in your hands, a hundred spines between us.

And all the things. Of these places. I am within. A without. Each time. Marks the text, scars tissue, parts a second, third, a fourth mouth from which the story leaves me, polishing the throat.

———

Small dislocations, memories suck their way to the surface only to be buckled back to the other side of remembering. I am within a wall of dark water. Holding the ledge of a bright cloth, it is pulled from me.

Having been raised by water, the body sees with the voice. It is contained by nothing. Floating, buoyant. Mutable. How sound can temporarily clothe this body. How it raises a series of locations through relation, through echo and recognition. At the beginning, two children walked away from a bay, and while walking, they unnamed places. But it wasn't two children, it was only one. Who became conjoined. A woman whose voice, in the shape of a body or book, stood beside her.

―――

What is after the run-off. The island of the child's body. Where it was conceived and how. Over again. Its voice, receding, erodes the body while simultaneously delivering it.

These are notes on its detritus, the silt built-up in the mouth, unsilted across the page. To have left something, willingly.

Language as a conveyance of debris. Rendering the disassociation. The silence that sound has had to comprehend. At some invisible level. Below the logic most obviously conveyed through the line—this tidy sentence. Within its muscle memory of syllable contracting sound against syllable—a heritage of absence taken in, in order to carry on.

Where language tried to till a void. To erase something by creating a casing of sound. All moments when a word could not cleave her. She thinks *reparation*. She thinks *proliferation*. And the bifurcations of a self across lifetimes.

Through the process of writing, within the practice of reading, language reverberates. Never really arriving, yet having already, always in the process of a disassociated present. A tilted recognition, within which, if we are lucky, we are left with the feeling of having been. Of having had the idea of our skin, touched. Even if by our own hand returning to us from somewhere else.

———

The way grief pools until it can no longer contain its own accumulation. Grief in the place of absence as a result of silence. A secret even language couldn't see, impresses. This book to release a series of traces hemmed in to the nervous system, webbed across generations. To let silence into speech into shape. And then, to walk out, regardless.

That man, stepping off a bus, at daybreak, during a snowstorm, gave me to myself as if for the first time. Today he is six years into a thirty-year sentence. I wanted his hands severed. And yet, he started the relief of some unspeakable residual thing. I was able to shiver it off, for the first time, through a body made physical by his having breached it. I am coming to understand. This is not the event I can't write.

———

The distance between silence and language holds the body, which breathes, despite the consequences.

A child born at sea level will have a smaller lung capacity than a child born at higher altitudes.

During pregnancy, a mother's lung capacity decreases due to compression of the diaphragm imposed by the baby's weight. My whole life, I have been waiting to give birth to my own mother. Though she's been on the outside of my organs, I've carried her, heavy as a skull, at the bottom of me. As a child, I saw my mother cradle her own womb when sick, calling out to her mother, deceased five years by then.

Our organs are emotive. Lungs convert into satchels of grief. Dear Reader, our diaphragms contract, pulling. All this at once. And breathing requires no effort unless you are performing a physical activity. Reading is physical. Your air is in my lungs and you're picking me up. You're laying me out. You're letting me. Dear Reader, I wonder at how you are doing. What you have been filling yourself with. I've been moving through something and I've been so lonely. And then this, your reading, and all nights and through it all I think someone is here touching my knee or elbow. The back of my arm, leaning into me. And parts of me dissolve. *There's the body over there*, I think. *And here's my voice.* I don't want any of it sometimes. As if my body is a bowl or a reflecting mirror, wet, concave and moving toward a kind of transparency.

I can feel myself acclimating to you. I come here, to the space of the page because I want you. It's that simple, I think.

I'm so tired now. Every night I want to finish this book, send your letters off in the morning. It is night here. Becoming quiet now. A friend just left. I think of you and imagine what it might be like to be a friend of yours. In proximity. What might it mean for you to be able to come over to my house for a spontaneous dinner. Talking, sprawling across the couch and floor, pulling books from the shelf, laughing into them. What if when we talked I could touch your forearm for a moment. Brush your hair behind your shoulder. If I could see your whole self. If I could pull you to me before you left to hold you for half a minute. To say to you, *call me so I know you got home okay.*

———

I no longer want to contain my own erasures. I want to rid the book of myself, to rid the book from myself. I want my own vacancy. I want my body as a glass carafe, elegant as an eyelash, and completely without lineage.

I want my body's translucency, at once soft and crystalline, prismatic. To experience my voice, housed, sagely, as some slow electric current mobilizing the body through which it courses. I want to wash the numbness. To leave something reflective in its place. To take my name and turn its edges round and stable.

————

In December of 2011, after years away, I brought this book home with the intention to forgive the island that raised me. I wanted my own intentional dispersal. I wanted reincorporation. Between the place of me and my birth. To let our dialects contract, overlap, and set something clean.

I took this book to the Sound and I thought, *I'll just get it a little wet, let it warp and blur.* I wanted it saturated in salt and sand, all the sediment of the island. Secretly, I wanted to beat it into a pulp, to take up its shredded, wet body like something disemboweled, and to make a new kind of paper with it. Walk into the winter bay and maybe come out as something else or maybe not come out at all, just be taken up like light, but I was too afraid to do any of those things. I was afraid because I thought if I began, I wouldn't be able to stop, I'd just go on in that way until there was nothing left of myself or the pages. So I knelt, anchored the book with two rocks, and began to dig.

Soon, I had a cavity large enough and a pile of stones. I made a threshold of rocks around the ledge of the hollow. I put my face into it. Felt the damp rising to meet me. I spoke my book's title into the mouth. Made a small nest of dry seaweeds and tore my biography from the back of my manuscript. I didn't want to bury the book, just the parts of myself that were blocking the book's arrival. The parts that were too self-conscious: the author, the academic. I wanted to remember my own originating form, like a perfect, impossible sound finally found and uttered, shared with someone else as a bridge of light between bodies. It was the history of myself in all my possible forms that I wanted. I wanted to write from a limitless place, not the place I had become through my fear. So I made a noise outside of language, a series of sounds, and I tore the sentences about myself into strands, wove them into the weeds, and set it to fire. Soon, it went to ash and I buried the remains, leaving the circle of stones.

I was alone on the winter beach except for a colony of gulls overhead and a few scattered plovers at the bearded edge of the sand. I took this book, the unbound manuscript, and crouched where the surf completed its extension and reversed itself. I held the book underwater. I wanted the bay to teach me what my voice could not understand. To watch my book, waterlogged, touched, take on an unrecognizable shape.

Holding the book firmly in my hands, the water kept arriving. I watched the pages bloat, distend, and bow under the wave's direction, until the whole of it was suddenly pulled away from me with the surf.

I could do nothing but let it be taken. I watched the book rear against the muscle of the water. It seemed a living organism that had unexpectedly arrived at shore. Lit and algae-colored, the sea flexed and released, separating the book into sheets until its form was over six feet in length, its body opening like an accordion parallel to the coastline. This happened slowly, just feet below the bay's surface, and somehow the book was held near-stationary by converging currents. It appeared as an elongated ghost and remained suspended, slowly rotating, for many minutes. It let me watch, and I felt myself as weightless as it had become.

———

That night, as my book was being washed between water and island, I dreamed myself housed in a residence of sand—the floor, the walls, a cradle or kiva wherein I could hear the sand's minutial movements.

And then, in that way a dream can abruptly break its continuity, the scene spliced and I saw myself doubled. She was sitting, knees folded to her side, looking landward, cradled by a shallow depression of beach. In her hands she held a long linen curtain. She was embroidering our name over and over into the weave.

There is no need, she said to me from somewhere that was not her voice, but some silent consciousness between us. I wanted to believe her—that maybe this book would no longer need to be written and read. To have resigned myself—the eight years of writing, the thirty years of living—to the earth, all loam and vegetation. That place where the waters converge, where an island erodes and sediments.

And I saw myself kneel in front of this second self. I took her, let her drape us in her cloth, and we leaned over into the sand to rest.

———

The next morning, I returned to the beach. I trailed the shore in the direction the current and tide should have carried my book. I crouched down. I swept my hands over the sand trying to detect something. I kept coming up with flecks of seaweed. After an hour, I was cold. It was just days before January and I felt foolish for looking for something that had been taken, washed off. I thought I would find something given back to me. Some part of my book washed up, beached and waiting, wanting me.

I was thinking to leave when a cluster of gulls took off into the wind and hovered; I sat down to watch them. I remembered my doubled self from the dream and leaned over to lie on the beach. And after a while my pupils adjusted to the light. I could see the sun ignite tiny shards of ink. From that angle, all these miniscule scales of paper flared. This dispersal extended dozens of feet in both directions. Fins of paper were woven into the knotted kelp and sea lettuces, shingled upon rocks, mollusks, and clamshells, pulped and reincorporated into the beach's debris.

Danielle Vogel is a poet, lyric essayist, and installation artist whose work explores the bonds between language and presence, between a reader and a writer, and how a book—as an extended architecture of a body—might serve as a site of radical transformation. She is the author of *Edges & Fray* (Wesleyan, 2020) and *Between Grammars* (Noemi, 2015). Her installations, or "public ceremonies for language," have been most recently exhibited at RISD Museum, MICA, the University of Arizona's Poetry Center, and Abecedarian Gallery. She teaches at Wesleyan University and makes her home in New England with the artist Renee Gladman.